REVISED EDITION

Vocal Solo
KIDS' BROADWAY SONGBOOK
SONGS ORIGINALLY SUNG ON STAGE BY CHILDREN

CONTENTS

ANNIE	8	It's the Hard-Knock Life[2]
	5	Maybe[2]
	12	Tomorrow[2]
ANNIE WARBUCKS	2	I Always Knew[2]
A CHRISTMAS STORY	16	Red Ryder® Carbine Action BB Gun[3]
GYPSY	22	Let Me Entertain You[3]
INTO THE WOODS	25	I Know Things Now[4]
	30	Into the Woods[1]
THE KING AND I	36	I Whistle a Happy Tune[2]
MAME	41	My Best Girl (My Best Beau)[5]
MATILDA THE MUSICAL	54	Naughty[3]
	48	When I Grow Up[3]
THE ME NOBODY KNOWS	44	The Tree[2]
LES MISÉRABLES	68	Castle on a Cloud[2]
THE MUSIC MAN	65	Gary, Indiana[2]
OLIVER!	76	Where Is Love?[2]
	78	Who Will Buy?[2]
RUTHLESS	71	Born to Entertain[2]
THE SECRET GARDEN	82	The Girl I Mean to Be[2]
SHENANDOAH	85	Why Am I Me?[2]
SOUTH PACIFIC	92	Dites-Moi (Tell Me Why)[2]

Pianists on the recordings: [1]Brendan Fox, [2]Louise Lerch, [3]John Reed, [4]Richard Walters, [5]Lawrence Yurman

To access companion recorded accompaniments online, visit:
www.halleonard.com/mylibrary

Enter Code
5783-5151-6351-9218

ISBN: 978-0-634-03065-9

7777 W. BLUEMOUND RD. P.O. BOX 13819 MILWAUKEE, WI 53213

For all works contained herein:
Unauthorized copying, arranging, adapting, recording, Internet posting, public performance,
or other distribution of the printed music in this publication is an infringement of copyright.
Infringers are liable under the law.

Visit Hal Leonard Online at
www.halleonard.com

MAYBE
from the Musical Production *Annie*

Lyric by Martin Charnin
Music by Charles Strouse

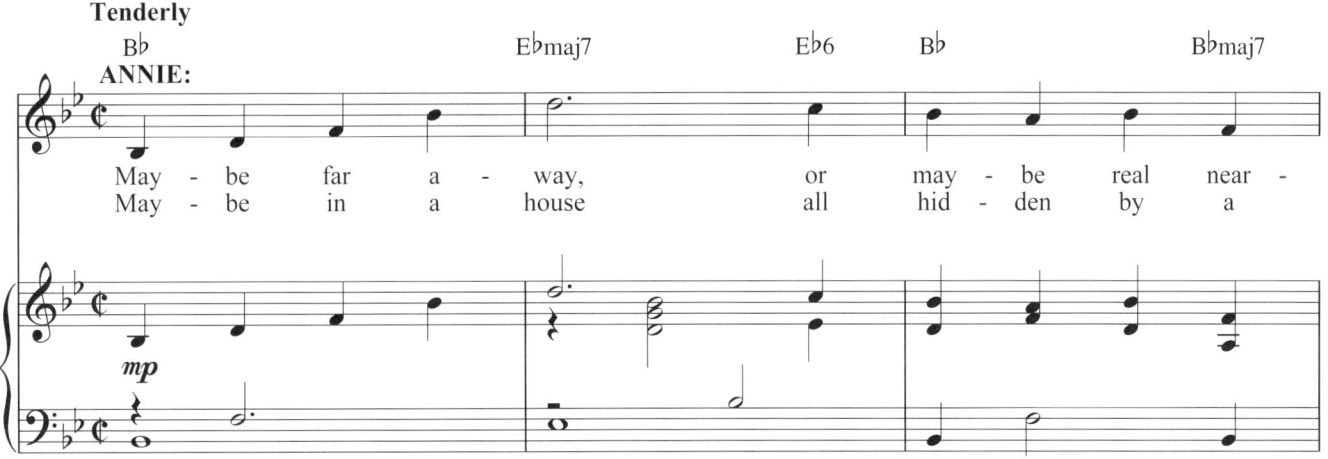

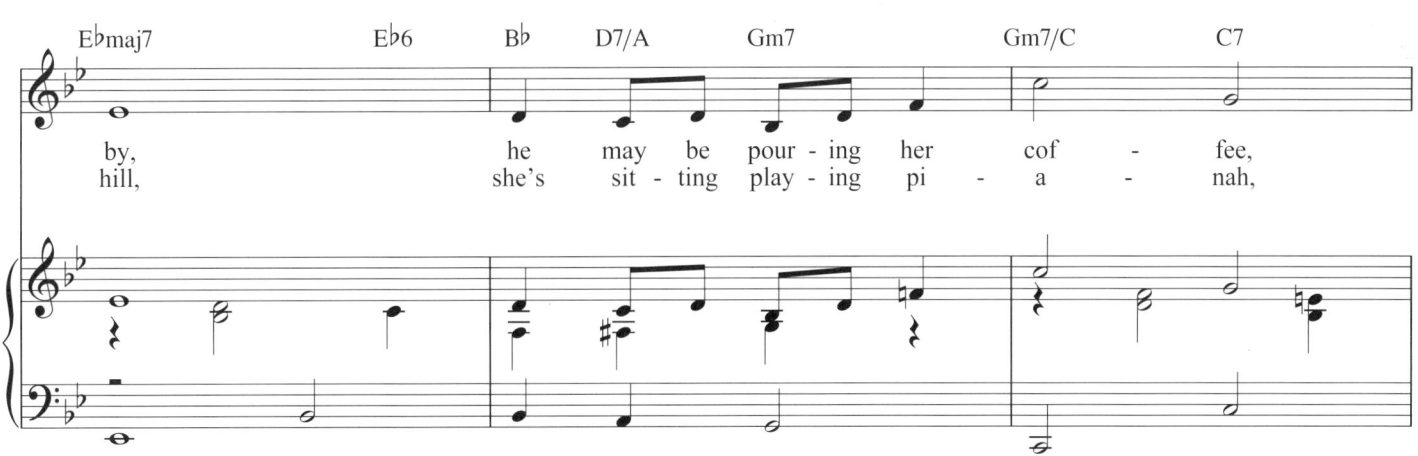

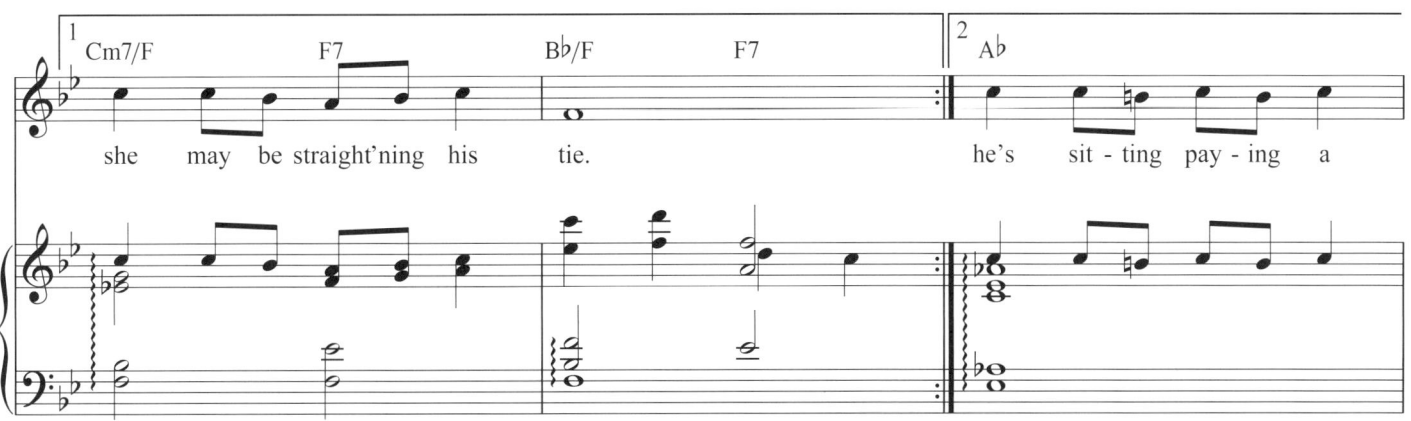

© 1977 (Renewed) EDWIN H. MORRIS & COMPANY, A Division of MPL Music Publishing, Inc. and CHARLES STROUSE PUBLISHING
All Rights for CHARLES STROUSE PUBLISHING Administered by WB MUSIC CORP.
All Rights Reserved   Used by Permission

IT'S THE HARD-KNOCK LIFE
from the Musical Production *Annie*

Lyric by Martin Charnin
Music by Charles Strouse

This song is performed by Annie and The Orphans in the show, adapted here as a solo for Annie.

© 1977 (Renewed) EDWIN H. MORRIS & COMPANY, A Division of MPL Music Publishing, Inc. and CHARLES STROUSE PUBLISHING
All Rights for CHARLES STROUSE PUBLISHING Administered by WB MUSIC CORP.
All Rights Reserved   Used by Permission

RED RYDER® CARBINE ACTION BB GUN

from *A Christmas Story - The Musical*

Words and Music by Benj Pasek
and Justin Paul

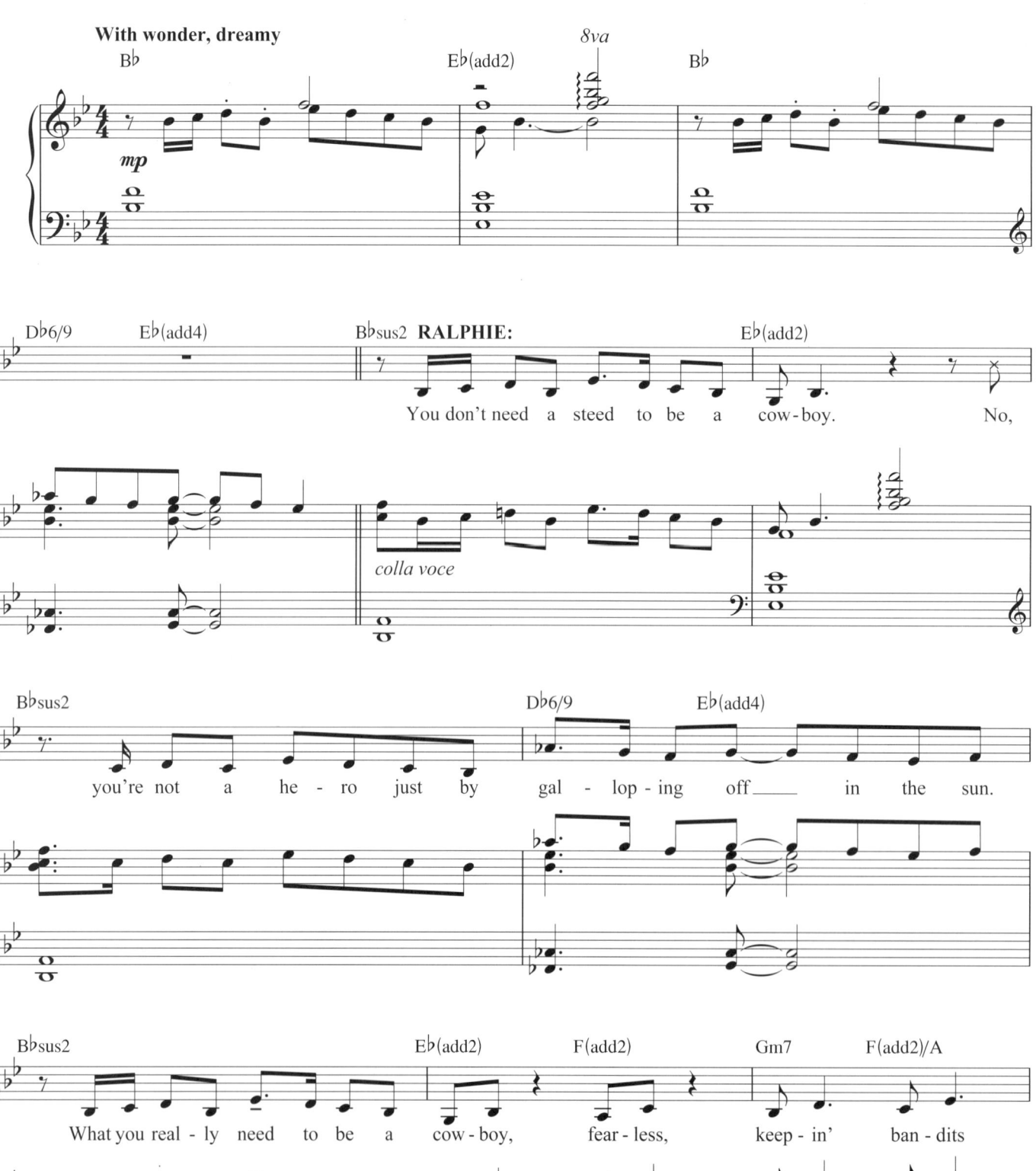

This song is performed by June and Louise in the show, adapted here as a solo for June.

I KNOW THINGS NOW
from *Into The Woods*

Words and Music by
Stephen Sondheim

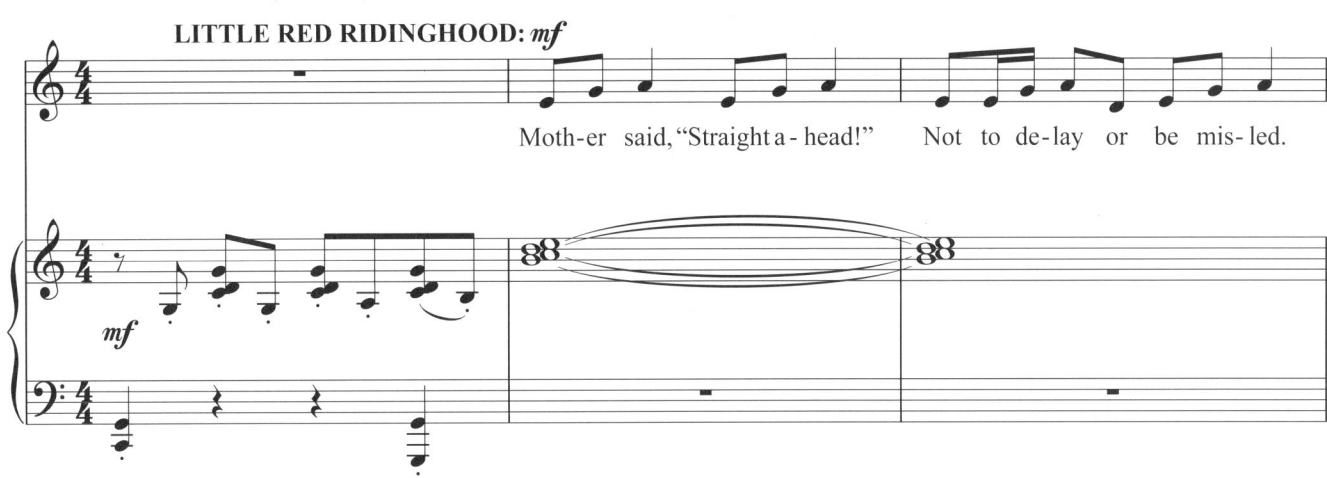

© 1988 RILTING MUSIC, INC.
All Rights Administered by WB MUSIC CORP.
All Rights Reserved   Used by Permission

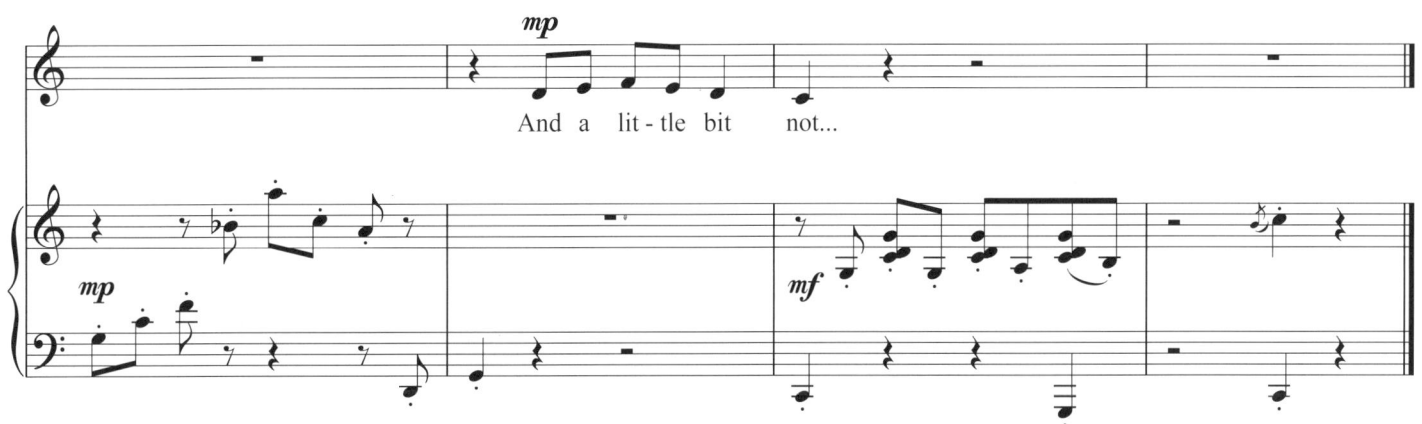

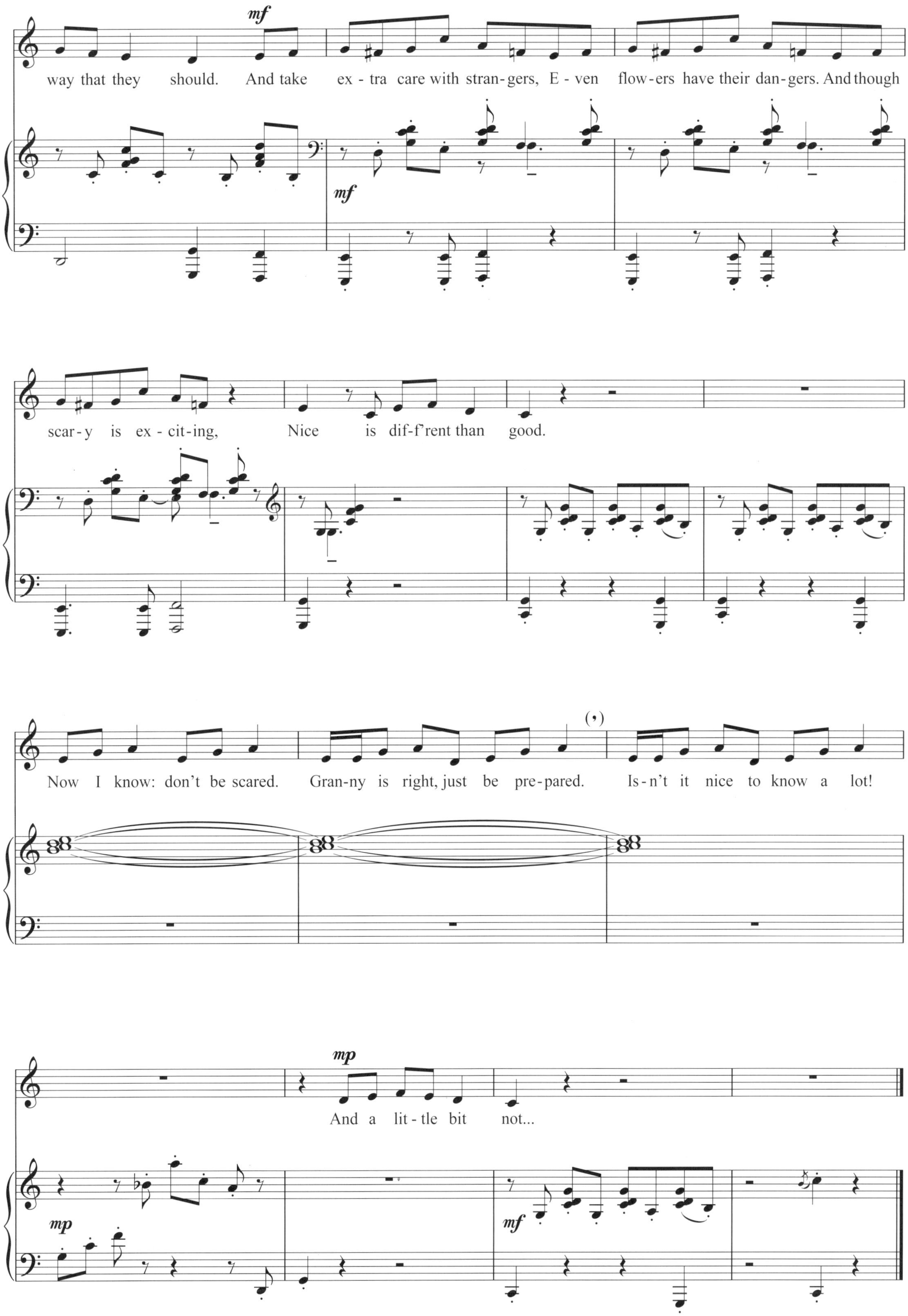
mf
way that they should. And take ex - tra care with stran - gers, E - ven flow - ers have their dan - gers. And though
mf
scar - y is ex - cit - ing, Nice is dif - f'rent than good.
Now I know: don't be scared. Gran - ny is right, just be pre - pared. Is - n't it nice to know a lot!
mp
And a lit - tle bit not...
mp
mf

INTO THE WOODS
from *Into the Woods*

Words and Music by
Stephen Sondheim

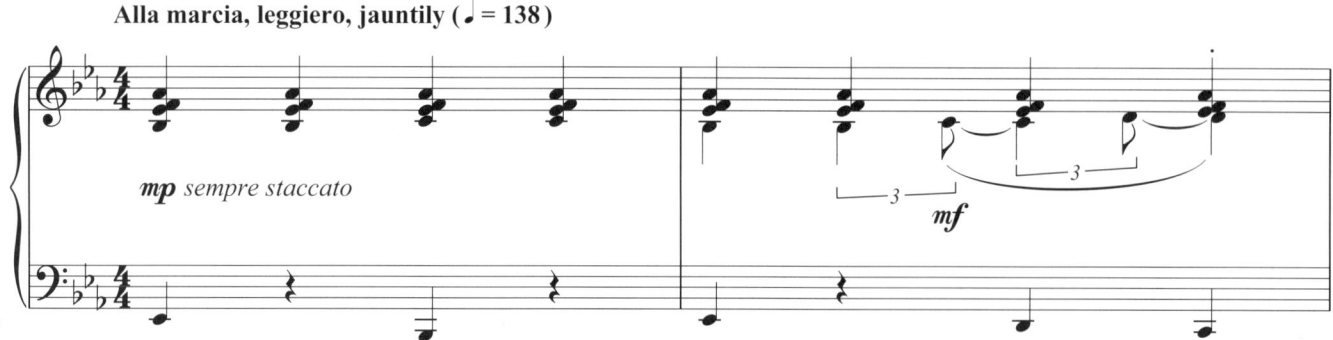

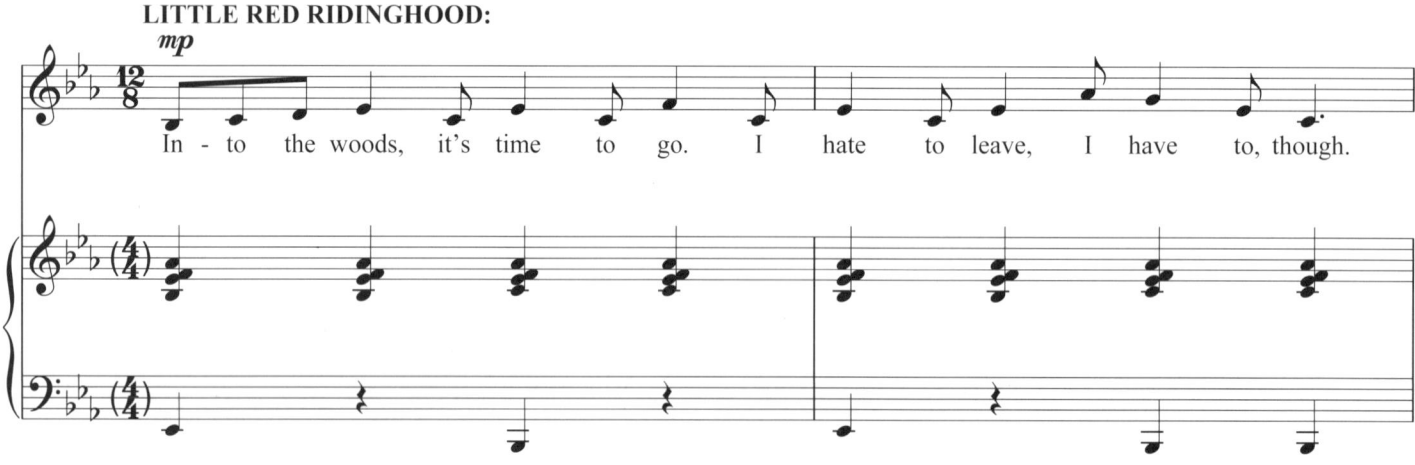

© 1988 RILTING MUSIC, INC.
All Rights Administered by WB MUSIC CORP.
All Rights Reserved   Used by Permission

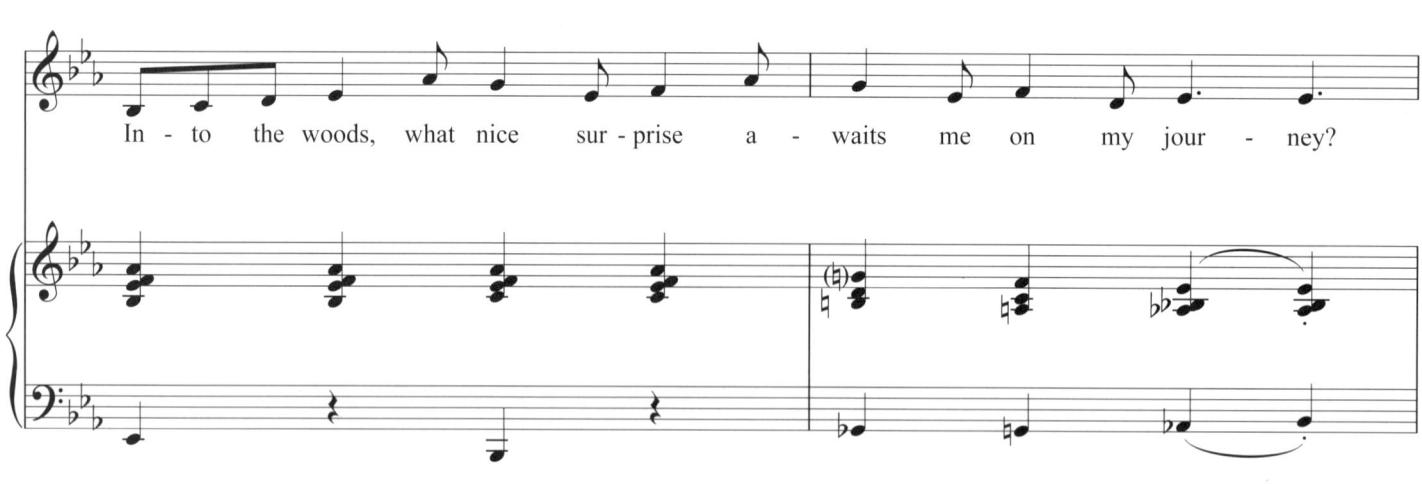

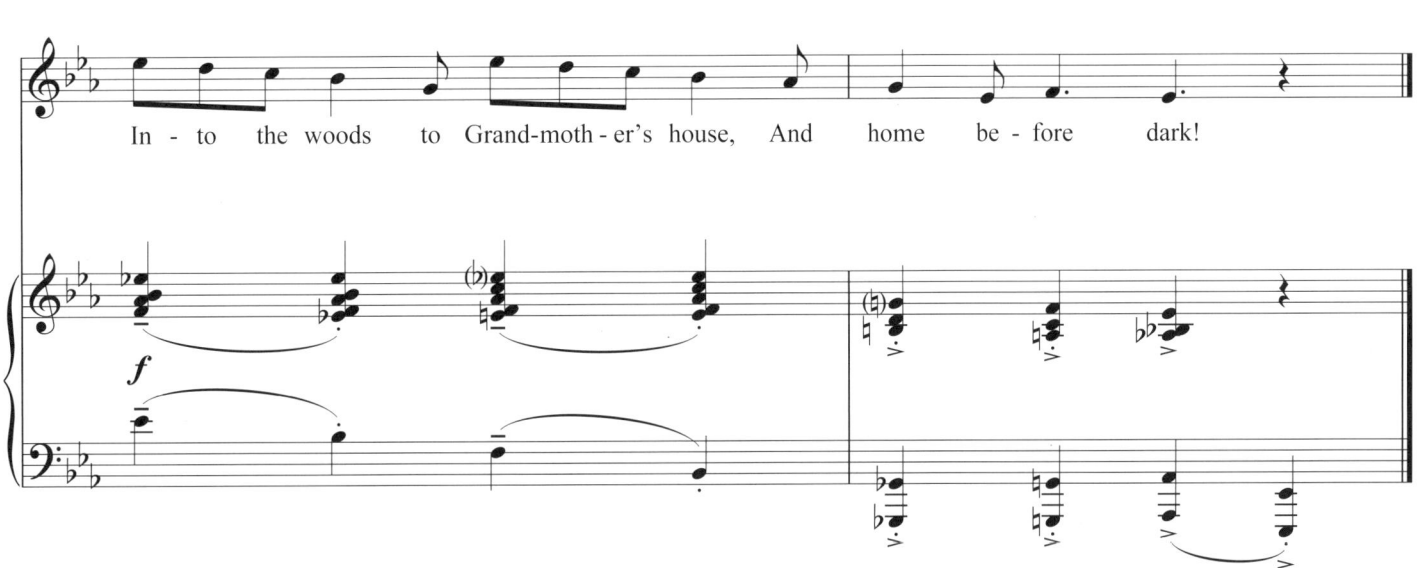

I WHISTLE A HAPPY TUNE

from *The King and I*

Lyrics by Oscar Hammerstein II
Music by Richard Rodgers

This song is performed by Anna and Louis Leonowens in the show, adapted here as a solo.

Copyright © 1951 by Richard Rodgers and Oscar Hammerstein II
Copyright Renewed
Williamson Music, a Division of Rodgers & Hammerstein: an Imagem Company, owner of publication and allied rights throughout the world
International Copyright Secured   All Rights Reserved

fraid. While shiv-er-ing in my shoes I strike a care-less pose And whis-tle a hap-py tune, And no one ev-er knows I'm a-fraid. The re-

G♭ G♭6 B♭
sult of this de - cep - tion is ver - y strange to
B♭6 F/C Fm6/C
tell For when I fool the peo - ple I fear, I
C7 F7 B♭
fool my - self as well! I whis - tle a hap - py
B♭9 E♭ E♭maj7 E♭6
tune And ev - 'ry sin - gle time The
p

hap-pi-ness in the tune con-vinc-es me that I'm not a-fraid.

Coda

Make be-lieve you're brave And the trick will take you far.

You may be as brave as you make be-lieve you

are. *Whistle* _____

You may be as brave as you make be-lieve you are. _____

MY BEST GIRL (MY BEST BEAU)
from *Mame*

Music and Lyric by Jerry Herman
Arranged by Michael Dansicker

Moderate Waltz

You're my best girl and nothing you do is
(beau)*
wrong, I'm proud you belong to me; And if a day is rough for me, Having you there's enough for me. And if someday an-

---

* This may be used as a substitute throughout.
This song is performed by Patrick and Mame Dennis in the show, adapted here as a solo.

© 1966 (Renewed) JERRY HERMAN
All Rights Controlled by JERRYCO MUSIC CO.
Exclusive Agent: EDWIN H. MORRIS & COMPANY, A Division of MPL Music Publishing, Inc.
All Rights Reserved

oth-er girl comes a-long, It won't take her long to see, That I'll still be found just hang-in' a-round My best girl. And if some-day an-oth-er girl comes a-

F7(♭5) F7 B♭ Gm C9 Am D7
long, It won't take her long to see, That
Gm Cm7(♭5) G♭+/D E♭m B♭+/F
I'll still be found just hang-in' a - round My
Fsus4 F7 Gm Cm7 Gm/D Cm B♭+/F Fsus4 F7
best girl! My best
rall.
mp poco rit.
B♭ Dm Cm7 F7 B♭
girl.
a tempo
rall.

THE TREE
from *The Me Nobody Knows*

Lyric by Will Holt
Music by Gary William Friedman

Freely

This man I know has an apple tree he's hoping will grow day after day he waits and what does he see

Copyright © 1970 by Alley Music Corp. and Trio Music Company
Copyright Renewed
All Rights for Trio Music Company Administered by BMG Rights Management (US) LLC
International Copyright Secured   All Rights Reserved
Used by Permission

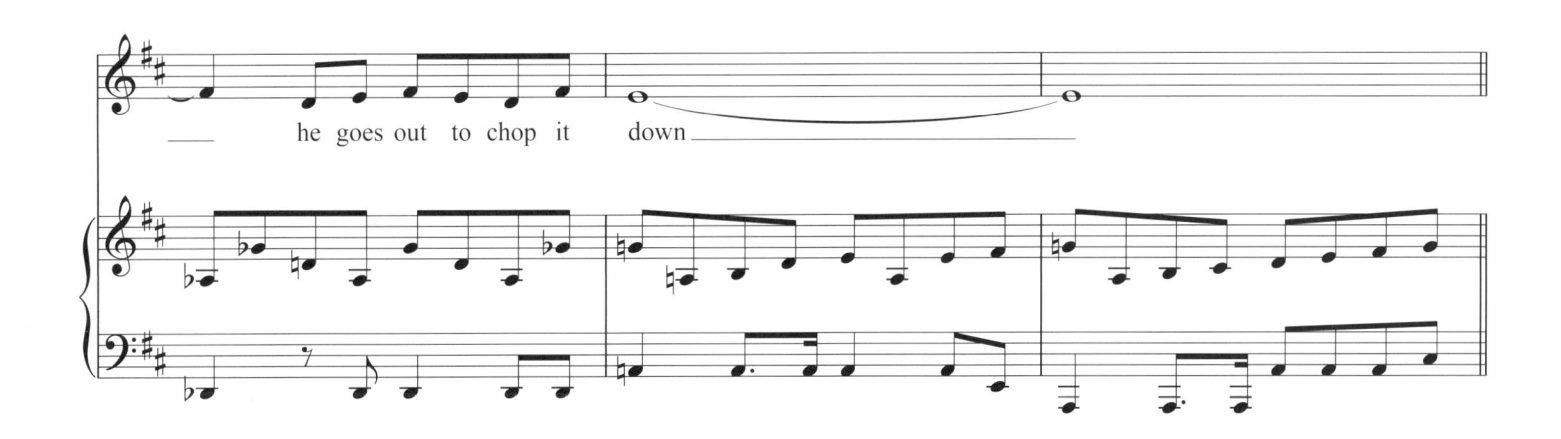

not one ap-ple on the tree

rit.

Moderately

This man I know works all win-ter but the tree will not grow

a tempo

till late in Spring with still no fruit to be found

he goes out to chop it down

Lo and behold_____ like a miracle swept in from the sea_____ Lo and behold_____ there's a fog so thick the man can't see to cut the tree._ Next morning he_____ all excited he comes

run - nin' to me _____ right there for all to see way
up on a bough _____ small and weak but hang - in'
on some - how _____ is a ba - by ap - ple
now. _____

rit.

WHEN I GROW UP
from *Matilda the Musical*

Words and Music by
Tim Minchin

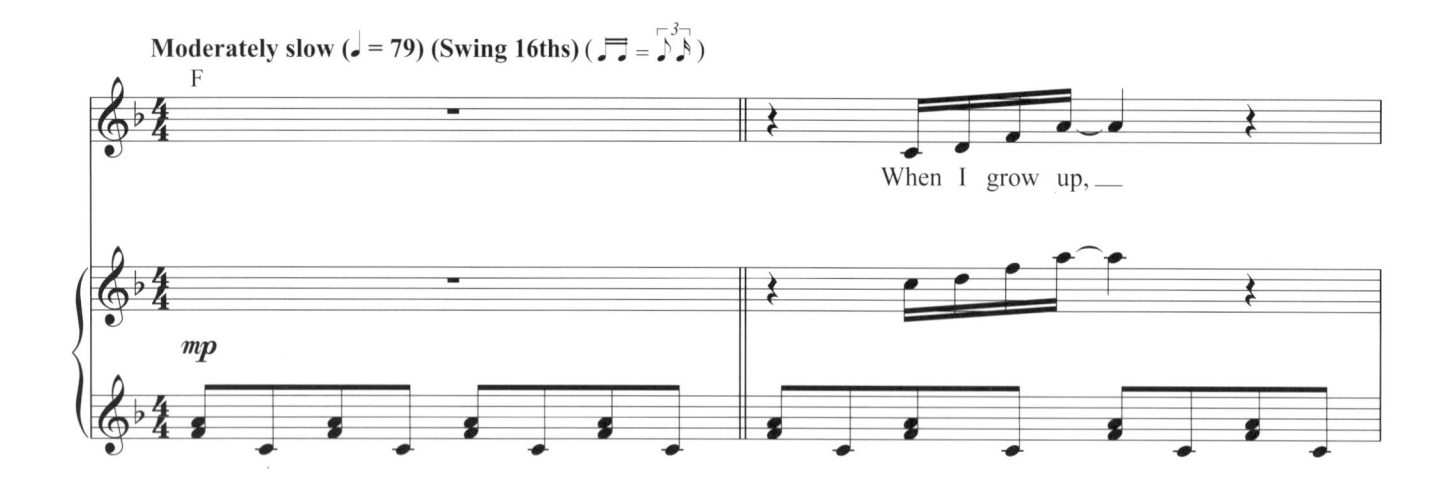

Moderately slow (♩ = 79) (Swing 16ths)

When I grow up,

I will be tall enough to reach the branches that I need to reach to climb the trees you get to climb when you're grown

© Copyright 2011 Navel Enterprises Pty Ltd./Kobalt Music Publishing Limited
Print rights for the world exclusively administered by Music Sales Limited
All Rights Reserved   International Copyright Secured

up. And when I grow up,

I will be smart enough to answer all the questions that you need to know the answers to before you're grown up.

And when I grow up I will

eat sweets ev-'ry day on the way to work and I will go to bed late ev-'ry night. And I will wake up when the sun comes up and I will watch car-toons un-til my eyes go square and I won't care 'cause I'll be all grown up when I grow up.

When I grow up, when I grow up, I will be strong enough to carry all the heavy things you have to haul around with you when you're a grown up.

F
And when I grow up,
C
when I grow up. I will be
3
B♭maj7
brave e - nough to fight the crea - tures
Gm7♭5
that you have to fight be - neath the bed
F
C/E
C
each night to be a grown up.
B♭(add9)
And when I grow up,
B♭(add9)
I will
F/A
have treats ev - 'ry day and I'll play

with things that Mum pretends that mums don't think are fun. And I will wake up, when the sun comes up and I will spend all day just lying in the sun and I won't burn 'cause I'll be all grown up when I grow up.

NAUGHTY
from *Matilda the Musical*

Words and Music by
Tim Minchin

Swing (♩ = c. 140)

MATILDA:

Jack and Jill went up the hill to fetch a pail of water, so they say. The sub-se-quent fall was in-ev-i-ta-ble. They nev-er stood a chance. They were writ-ten that way. In-no-cent vic-tims of their sto-ry. Like

© Copyright 2011 Navel Enterprises Pty Ltd./Kobalt Music Publishing Limited
Print rights for the world exclusively administered by Music Sales Limited
All Rights Reserved   International Copyright Secured

Ro-me-o and Ju-li-et: 'twas writ-ten in the stars be-fore they e-ven met that love and fate and a touch of stu-pid-i-ty would rob them of their hope of liv-ing hap-pi-ly. The end-ings are of-ten a lit-tle bit go-ry. *(Finger snaps)* I won-der why they did-n't just change their sto-ry.

We're told we have to do what we're told, but sure-ly some-times you have to be a lit-tle bit naugh-ty. Just be-cause you find that life's not fair, it does-n't mean that you just have to grin and bear it. If you al-ways take it on the

57

chin and wear it, nothing will change.

E-ven if you're lit-tle you can do a lot,___ you must-n't let a lit-tle thing like lit-tle stop___ you. If you sit a-round___ and let them get on top,___ you might as well be say-ing you think that it's o-kay, and that's not right!!

Cin-der-el-la, in the cel-lar, did-n't have to do much as far as I could tell. Her God-moth-er was two-thirds fair-y, sud-den-ly her lot was a lot less scar-y. But what if you have-n't got a fair-y to fix it?

Sometimes you have to make a little bit of mischief!

Just because you find that life's not fair, it doesn't mean that you just have to grin and bear it.

If you always take it on the chin and wear it, nothing will change.

Even if you're little you can do a lot, you mustn't let a little thing like little stop you. If you sit around and let them get on top, you might as well be saying you think that it's okay, and that's not right! And if it's not right, you have to put it right.

In the slip of a bolt, there's a ti-ny re-volt. The see of a war in the creak of a floor-board. A storm can be-gin with the flap of a wing. The ti-ni-est mite packs the might-i-est sting. Ev-'ry day starts with the tick__ of a clock.__ All es-capes start with a click__ of a lock.__

If you're stuck__ in your sto-ry and want to get out,__ you don't have to cry,__

__ you don't have to shout!__ 'Cause if you're lit-tle, you can do a lot,__ you must-

-n't let a lit-tle thing like lit-tle stop__ you. If you sit a-round and let them

get on top,__ you won't change a thing.

Just be-cause you find that life's not fair, it does-n't mean that you just have to grin and bear_ it. If you al-ways take it on the chin and wear it, you might as well be say-ing you think that it's o-kay, and that's not right!

N.C. Dm C/E F Dm
And if it's not right, you have to put it
E7 A7 Gm7
right. But no - bod - y else is gon - na
C7 Am7♭5 D7
put it right for me. No - bod - y but me is gon - na change my sto - ry.
Gm7 C F N.C. F
Some-times you have to be a lit - tle bit naugh - ty.

GARY, INDIANA
from Meredith Willson's *The Music Man*

By Meredith Willson

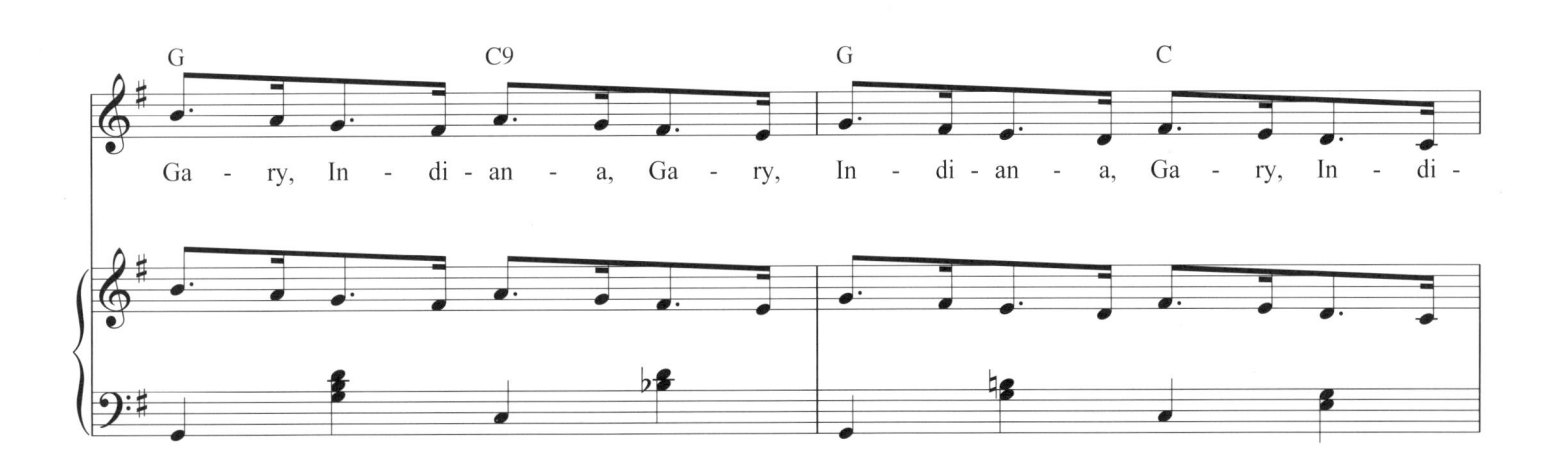

Soft-Shoe bounce

Ga - ry, In - di - an - a, Ga - ry, In - di - an - a, Ga - ry, In - di - an - a, let me say it once a - gain. Ga - ry, In - di - an - a, Ga - ry, In - di - an - a, Ga - ry, In - di -

© 1954, 1957, 1958, 1959 (Renewed) FRANK MUSIC CORP. and MEREDITH WILLSON MUSIC
All Rights Reserved

an - a, that's the town that knew me when. If you'd like to have a log-i-cal ex-pla-na-tion how I hap-pened on this el-e-gant syn-co-pa-tion, I will say with-out a mo-ment of hes-i-ta-tion, there is

Bm Dm6 E7♯5 A Cm6 D7♯5 G C9
just one place that can light my face. Ga - ry, In - di-an - a, Ga - ry,
G C G D Bm7 Dm6 E7
In - di-an - a, not Lou-i - si - an - a, Par - is, France, New York or Rome, but
A9 D7
Ga - ry, In - di-an - a, Ga - ry, In - di-an - a, Ga - ry, In - di - an - a, my home sweet
1 G G7 2 G E♭7 G D7 G
home. If you'd home.
f

CASTLE ON A CLOUD
from *Les Misérables*

Music by Claude-Michel Schönberg
Lyrics by Alain Boublil, Jean-Marc Natel
and Herbert Kretzmer

COSETTE:
There is a cas-tle on a cloud.
There is a room that's full of toys.

I like to go there in my sleep.
There are a hun-dred boys and girls.

Music and French Lyrics Copyright © 1980 by Editions Musicales Alain Boublil
English Lyrics Copyright © 1986 by Alain Boublil Music Ltd. (ASCAP)
Mechanical and Publication Rights for the U.S.A. Administered by Alain Boublil Music Ltd. (ASCAP) c/o Spielman Koenigsberg & Parker LLP,
Richard Koenigsberg, 1745 Broadway, New York NY 10019, Tel 212-453-2500, Fax 212-453-2550, ABML@skpny.com
International Copyright Secured. All Rights Reserved. This music is copyright. Photocopying is illegal.
All Performance Rights Restricted.

Dm C/E E E+ F
Aren't an - y floors for me to sweep,
No - bod - y shouts or talks too loud,
Dm E
not in my cas - tle on a cloud.
not in my cas - tle on a
1
Am
2
Am
cloud.
F6 C
There is a la - dy all in white,
F C
holds me and sings a lull - a - by.
B♭ F
She's nice to see and she's soft to touch. She

E
says, "Co - sette, I love you ver - y much."
rall.
Am E F Dm E
I know a place where no one's
a tempo
Am
lost.
G
I know a place where no one
C
cries.
Dm C/E E E+
Cry - ing at all is not al -
F
lowed,
Dm E
not in my cas - tle on a
Am
cloud.
rall.

BORN TO ENTERTAIN
from *Ruthless*

Lyric by Joel Paley
Music by Marvin Laird

Moderate Swing

TINA: Some girls like to cook and sew; When I cook it's in a show. I was born to entertain.

spoken to audience: "How ya doin'?" Some girls prefer to

Copyright © 1992 by MARVY MUSIC (ASCAP)
All Rights Reserved   Used by Permission

Dm7 G13 Cmaj9 C/E Eb m6sus Dm9 A13(b9) Bm/A
help mom clean, I'd rath - er learn a dance rou - tine.
Dm9 D#dim7 Dm9 Dm7 G13 C Dm
I was born to en - ter - tain.
D#dim C9/E Gm9 F6 F#dim7 Ab7/Gb
spoken to audience: "Where ya from?"
In - stead of walk - in' I go f' - lap - pin',
Cmaj7/G C6/G Am7 D13 Am7
When I tap, I make it hap - pen. Mom says I have

D9 Dm9 G7
Broad-way on the brain.
3
Cmaj9 Am9 Dm7 G13 Cmaj7 E♭/A
3
Don't get too com - fy in that seat, When I strut my stuff you'll be
3
Dm7 A13(♭9) Dm7 D♯dim7 Dm7 G♯5
on your feet. I was born to sing and dance.
C6 A9 Dm7 G G♭9(♯11) F6/9 F(add2)
Not ev - 'ry show biz

*Pocatello (pronounced Pocatella) is a town in Idaho.

Edim7 Db/Ab Fm7b5 Cmaj7/F Db6/F Bb7#5
born to a - muse, From the tip of my nose to the tap of my shoes. So
Ebm9 Edim7 Db(add2)/F Db6 C7 Fdim7 Fm9b5
strike up the band, And hand me my hat and my cane,
Cb/Bb Bb9 D7#5 Ebm9 Edim7 Db(add2)/F Gbmaj7 G13#11 Ebm/Ab
'Cause I was born to en - ter -
Db7(#9) Db7/F Gb9 Gdim7 Db Cb Ab G Gb E C Db
tain.
gliss.

WHERE IS LOVE?
from the Broadway Musical *Oliver!*

Words and Music by
Lionel Bart

Slowly, but rhythmically

OLIVER:
Where is love? Does it fall from skies a-bove?
Is it un-der-neath the wil-low tree that I've been dream-ing of?
Where is she, who I close my eyes to see? Will I ev-er know the

© Copyright 1960 (Renewed), 1968 (Renewed) Lakeview Music Co., Ltd., London, England
TRO - Hollis Music, Inc., New York, controls all publication rights for the U.S.A. and Canada
International Copyright Secured
All Rights Reserved Including Public Performance For Profit
Used by Permission

*In the film, Oliver sings the italicized lyrics the second time.

WHO WILL BUY?
from the Broadway Musical *Oliver!*

Words and Music by
Lionel Bart

Brightly, in 2

Who will buy this wonderful morning? Such a sky you never did see.

© Copyright 1960 (Renewed), 1968 (Renewed) Lakeview Music Co., Ltd., London, England
TRO - Hollis Music, Inc., New York, controls all publication rights for the U.S.A. and Canada
International Copyright Secured
All Rights Reserved Including Public Performance For Profit
Used by Permission

Who will tie it up with a rib-bon, and put it in a box for me? So I can see it at my lei-sure when ev-er things go wrong, and I would

There'll nev-er be a day so sun-ny; it could not hap-pen twice. Where is the

keep it as a treas - ure to
man with all the mon - ey? It's

last my whole life long.
cheap at half the price!

Who will buy this won - der - ful feel - ing?

I'm so high, I swear I could fly.

Me, oh, my, I don't want to lose it, so what am I to do, to keep the sky so blue? There must be some-one who will buy.

buy.

THE GIRL I MEAN TO BE
from *The Secret Garden*

Lyrics by Marsha Norman
Music by Lucy Simon

no one sees my life inside Where I can make my plans and write them down so I can read them A place where I can bid my heart be still, and it will mind me A place where I can go when I am lost, and there I'll find me. I need a place to spend the day Where no one says to go or stay Where I can take my pen and draw the girl I mean to be.

WHY AM I ME?
from *Shenandoah*

Lyric by Peter Udell
Music by Gary Geld

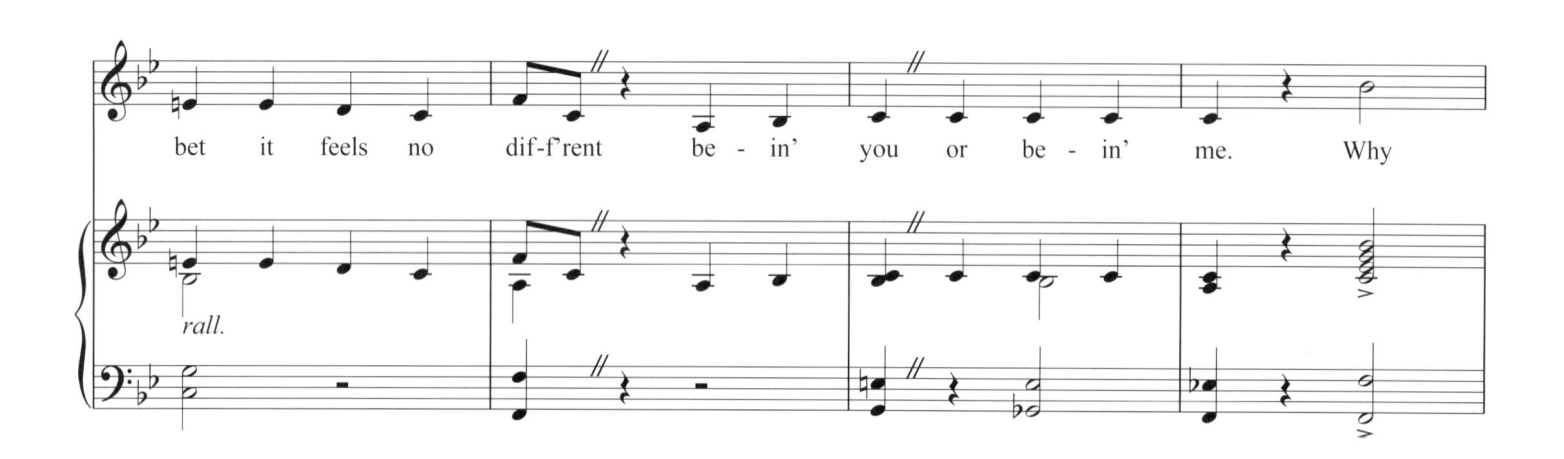

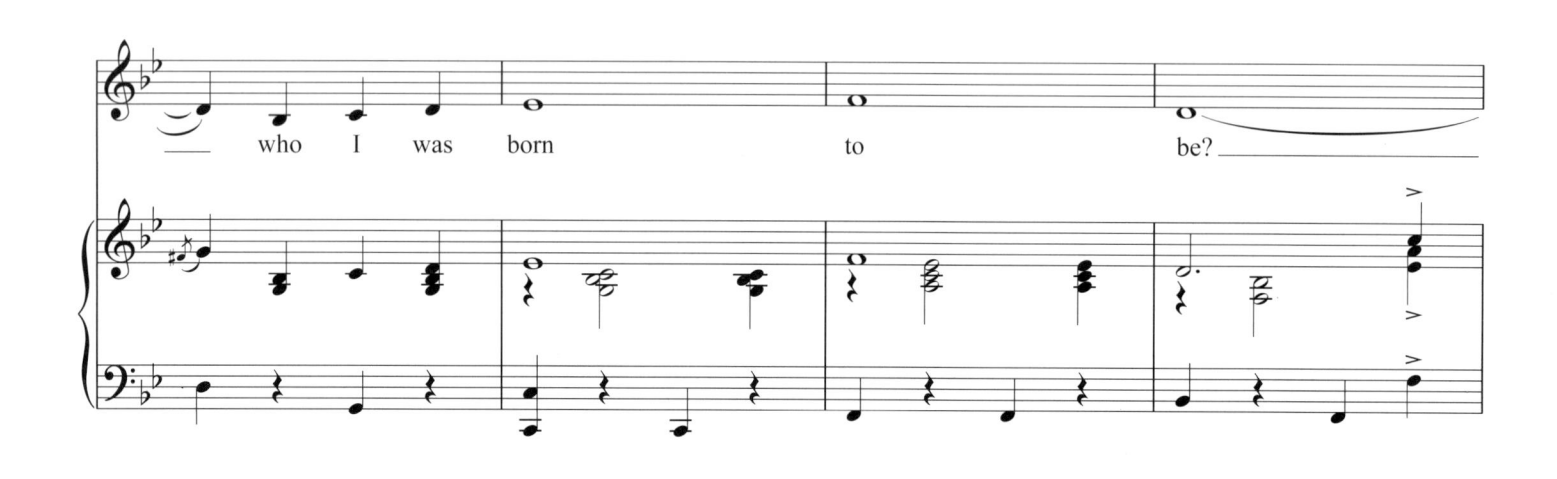

Way down un-der-neath it all,___ where no one gets to see, I'll bet it feels no dif-f'rent be-in' you or be-in' me. Why was I born?___ When I was born___ who I was born to be?___

Why was I given the body I'm livin' in?

Why am I Gabriel? Why am I Anderson?

Why am I me? Why am I me? Why am I me?

(Melody) Why am I here? Why am I now? Why am I

(Harmony) Why am I here? Why am I now? Why am I

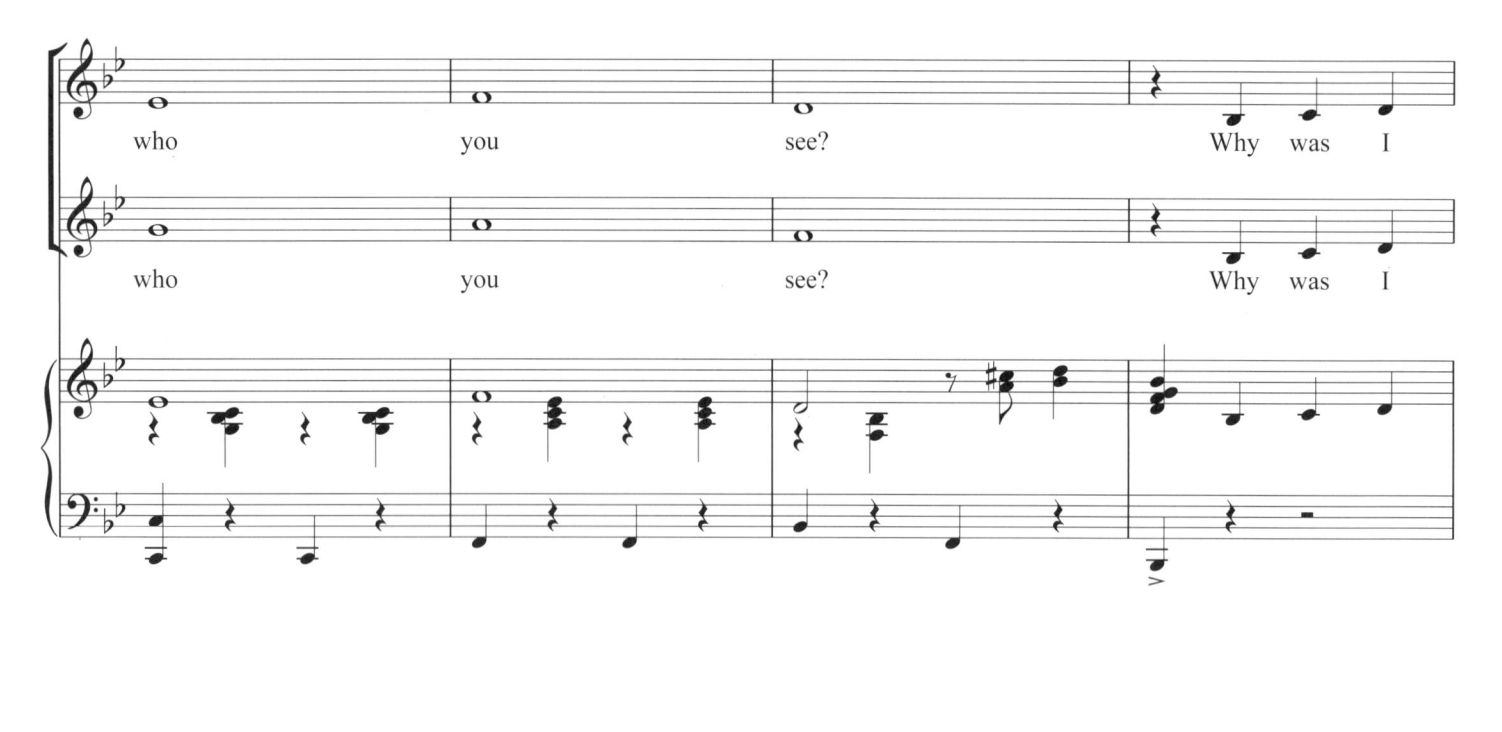

*who you see? Why was I
handed the person I landed in? Why am I
Gabriel? Why am I Anderson? Why am I me?*

Why am I me? Why am I me? I figure somebody puts the "who" into folks like droppin' a stone in a lake. So maybe I'm thinkin' I'm Abraham Lincoln and somebody made a mistake! if I were born _____ some-bod-y else _____ bet-cha I still would be me. So man-y be-ins' I know_ I could be me in. Why must I be in the be-in' you see me in?

Why am I An - der-son?
Why am I Ga - bri - el?
Why am I me? Why am I me? Why am I me? Why am I me?
Why am I me? Why am I me? Why am I me? Why am I me?
Why am I me? Why am I me?
Why am I me? Why am I me?
ff

DITES-MOI
(Tell Me Why)
from *South Pacific*

Lyrics by Oscar Hammerstein II
Music by Richard Rodgers

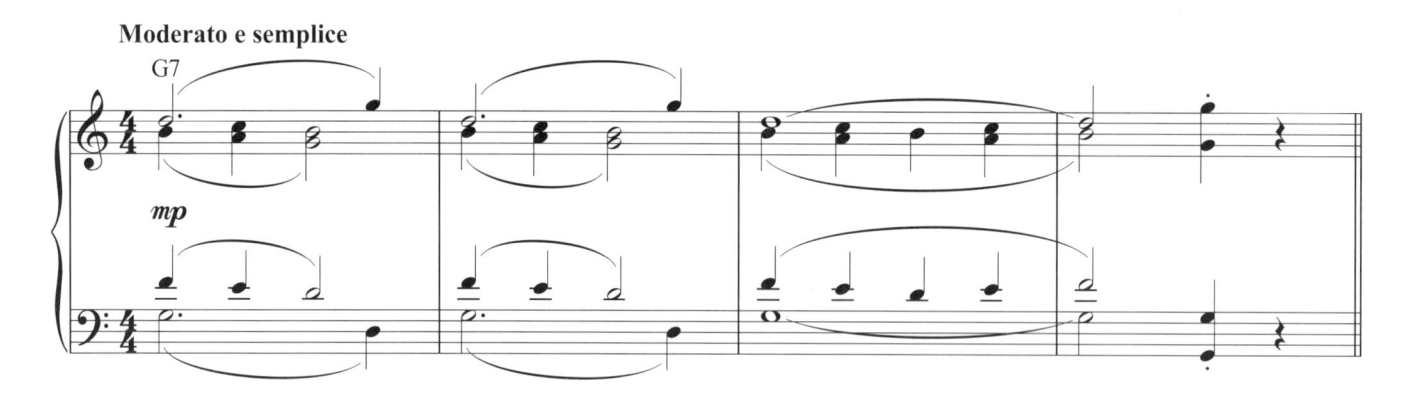

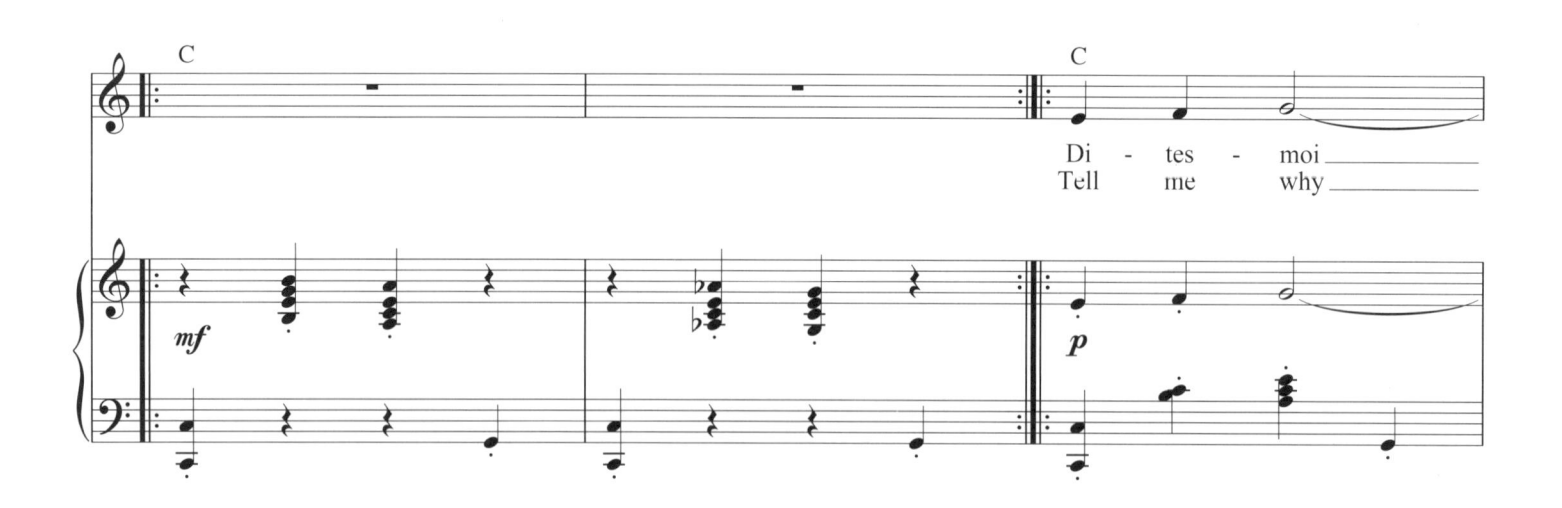

Moderato e semplice

Di- tes - moi _____ Pour- quoi _____ La vie est bel - le,
Tell me why _____ The sky _____ is filled with mu - sic,

Copyright © 1949 by Richard Rodgers and Oscar Hammerstein II
Copyright Renewed
Williamson Music, a Division of Rodgers & Hammerstein: an Imagem Company, owner of publication and allied rights throughout the world
International Copyright Secured   All Rights Reserved

Dites-moi ___ Pourquoi ___ La vie est
Tell me why ___ We fly ___ on clouds a-

gai? Dites-moi ___ Pourquoi,___
bove Can it be ___ that we ___

Chère ma-d'moi-sel - le, Est-ce-que
can fly to mu - sic Just be-cause,

poco rit. *delicat* **mp**

Par - ce que vous m'ai - mez? mez?
Just be-cause we're in love? love?

p